THESE T

THOSE LEAVES,

THIS FLOWER,

THAT FRUIT

ALSO BY HAYAN CHARARA

POETRY
Something Sinister
The Sadness of Others
The Alchemist's Diary

CHILDREN'S LITERATURE
The Three Lucys

ANTHOLOGY
Inclined to Speak (Editor)

THESE TREES,
THOSE LEAVES,
THIS FLOWER,
THAT FRUIT

poems

Hayan Charara

MILKWEED EDITIONS

Published 2022 by Milkweed Editions
Printed in the United States of America
Cover design by Mary Austin Speaker
22 23 24 25 26   6 5 4 3 2
First Edition

Library of Congress Cataloging-in-Publication Data

Names: Charara, Hayan, 1972- author.
Title: These trees, those leaves, this flower, that fruit : poems / Hayan Charara.
Description: First edition. | Minneapolis, Minnesota : Milkweed Editions, 2022. | Summary: "From Hayan Charara comes a candid new collection of poems, one that deconstructs the deceptively simple question of what it means to be good-a good person, a good citizen, a good teacher, a good poet, a good father"-- Provided by publisher.
Identifiers: LCCN 2021031227 (print) | LCCN 2021031228 (ebook) | ISBN 9781571315410 (trade paperback) | ISBN 9781571317520 (ebook)
Subjects: LCGFT: Poetry.
Classification: LCC PS3553.H316 T48 2022 (print) | LCC PS3553.H316 (ebook) | DDC 811/.54--dc23
LC record available at https://lccn.loc.gov/2021031227
LC ebook record available at https://lccn.loc.gov/2021031228

Milkweed Editions is committed to ecological stewardship. We strive to align our book production practices with this principle, and to reduce the impact of our operations in the environment. We are a member of the Green Press Initiative, a nonprofit coalition of publishers, manufacturers, and authors working to protect the world's endangered forests and conserve natural resources.

for R, and our children, J and A

CONTENTS

Self-Portrait in Retrospect • 1

Under the Sun • 2

Older • 6

Some Sentences • 7

Porch Haiku • 8

Elegy with Apples, Pomegranates, Bees, Butterflies, Thorn Bushes,
     Oak, Pine, Warblers, Crows, Ants, and Worms • 11

Neighbors • 13

Empathy • 14

Terrorism • 15

Self-Portrait as Trees • 20

On the Death of Other People's Children • 21

All These Questions You Ask • 22

Self-Portrait with Woman on the Subway • 24

The Problem with Me Is the Problem with You • 25

Unresolved Haiku

    Unresolved • 29

    Beautiful Morning • 29

    Being a Mother and Father • 29

    Getting By • 30

    How It Happened • 30

    Old Couple • 30

    Summertime • 31

    Seeing Our Mother Years After She Died • 31

    Condolence Then Apology • 31

    High School Angst, High School Tryst • 32

    The River in Winter • 32

    What Doesn't Kill You Makes You Stronger • 32

///

Prelude • 35

Fugue • 38

///

Self-Portrait after a Funeral • 49

Bees, Honeycombs, Honey • 50

The Symbolic Life • 53

Self-Portrait as Scientific Observation • 54

The Day Phil Levine Died • 56

The Prize • 59

Mean

    Sibling Rivalry • 64

    At the Party • 64

    To the Poet • 65

    Self-Portrait with Empty Pack of Cigarettes • 65

    Across the Country from a Cemetery in Michigan • 66

    Sincerity • 66

    Suddenly and Unexpectedly and from No Clearly
        Understood Cause • 66

Self-Portrait with Curses at 35,000 Feet • 67

Michigan • 69

The Night the Dog Died • 70

Self-Portrait with Dog, Possum, Newspaper, and Shovel • 71

The Other Woman • 72

Self-Portrait with Cassette Player • 73

Personal Political Poem • 74

Nothing Happened in 1999 • 76

That Summer That Year during the Heat Wave • 78

1979 • 79
Ode on an Abandoned House • 80
Apokaluptein • 81

///

Notes • 87
Acknowledgments • 91

THESE TREES,

THOSE LEAVES,

THIS FLOWER,

THAT FRUIT

SELF-PORTRAIT IN RETROSPECT

Young, I thought anger and shame
would in their own time
go away. God,
I was so beautiful then.

UNDER THE SUN

Which is holier,
the cathedral
burning

or the spiders
under the pews?
Is the match holy?

The phosphorus sesquisulfide,
the potassium chlorate,
the ammonium phosphate,

the paraffin wax,
the pine and ash,
or the pine and ash

set aflame?
And the moth
to the fire

or the butterfly
to the tree?
Which is holier,

the egg,
the caterpillar, the caterpillar
in the cocoon

in the chrysalis,
or the transmogrification?
Holy, holy.

Holy eyes, ears, mouth, nose.
Holy chin, cheeks, forehead.
Holy face, the face

loved as trees, leaves, bark, and roots
are loved.
Which is holier,

oak or linden?
The pleasure of the oak,
the sorrow of the linden.

Under a tree, a pecan,
a woman tells a joke,
the punchline

"donkey dick."
It is June, July, August.
Flies, mosquitoes, cicadas.

Humidity in the morning,
in the afternoon,
at sunset, midnight, dawn.

Holy day, holy night.
Holy flies, holy mosquitoes,
holy donkey.

Under a tree, a pine,
a leaf falls.
A thousand leaves fall.

Lobed, toothed, and untoothed.
Surrounded
by trees, a woman

remembers the fingers
touching her, the body
her fingers touched.

The sadness of joy,
the joy of sin.
The brilliance and astonishment

of a general proposition
weighed down
by the particular.

For better and worse.
Sin is like a tree, a leaf,
a flowering fruit.

Like these trees, those leaves,
this flower, that fruit.
In a paradisal garden,

which is holier,
the tree,
the fruit from the tree,

the woman eating
the fruit,
or the fruits of her labor?

In a garden
the pear thief mystic
hears a child, a girl or boy.

"Pick it up and read it."
"Pick it up and read it."
Is the fig holier than the body?

Is the acacia holier
than the mind?
The locust than memory?

Please pray
to the ginkgo, the poplar,
the sycamore.

Kneel before
the elm and alder.
Swear to the apple,

the plum, and the beech.
In the name of persimmon,
hemlock, and cypress,

in the name of ant,
mite, and beetle,
in the name of what drives us

to get up and look,
in the name of what saves us,
and what finishes us

at last.

OLDER

The dirt, damp with rain, is older than the sprouting grass.
And shadowing the grassy spikes, the oak trees
with brittle limbs that never fall
on the mailman walking across the lawn are older
than the house, and the house,
in a neighborhood once a forest, is older than the boy and girl
refusing to eat green beans—
they love candy, but less than they love
their mother. The girl is older than the boy,
the boy older than the cat, and the cat,
which cannot communicate
what it knows about age, hates
the cactuses on the windowsill—
a conqueror in the night, he paws and paws
and breaks, then marches
into the bedroom, across my stomach, and halts
on my chest—his warm breath and wet nose
young as the new moon, barely a crescent tonight,
twenty-two years after you died. O,
mother, I am older now than you ever would be.

SOME SENTENCES

A poet I loved and was betrayed by
loved me again and my ex-wife
took me to a hotel to fuck my brains out,
something we never did, but just as her body
touched mine a crowd of people appeared,
an acquaintance, a colleague,
my current wife, one by one defiling
the moment, the room, and then,
because they do not give a rat's ass
about daylight savings, my kids
woke me at 6 a.m., a false hour,
and the lawn needed mowing, the mower
needed gas, and halfway through I ran out
of leaf bags so I called the kids,
they had at the pile of leaves, and the air
smelled like a past I never had
yet always imagined as my own,
a past in which I go on listening
for the sentences never said.

PORCH HAIKU

On the porch
the men argue,
the cat sleeps.

On the porch—
we shut up for a minute
to hear cicadas.

On the porch
listening to the radio—
no survivors.

On the porch
I watch a dog
eat from the trash.

On the porch
the ashtray fills up
with rain.

On the porch
the neighbor waves, I wave back—
every goddamn day.

On the porch
the dog I named Saddam
wags its tail.

On the porch
the hajji sees me come home
drunk.

On the porch
the Fourth of July—
busy killing mosquitoes.

On the porch
I swat a fly, the neighbor
rolls grape leaves.

On the porch—
the streetlamps come on,
we keep grumbling.

On the porch—
we speak long-distance, I think,
for the last time.

On the porch
we tell each other
dirty jokes.

On the porch
a fly alights a teacup—
neither of us move.

On the porch,
hot, humid August—
a new war begins.

ELEGY WITH APPLES, POMEGRANATES, BEES, BUTTERFLIES, THORN BUSHES, OAK, PINE, WARBLERS, CROWS, ANTS, AND WORMS

The trees alongside the fence
bear fruit. The limbs and leaves, speeches
to you and me promising to give the world
back to itself. The apple apologizes
for those whose hearts bear too much zest
for heaven, the pomegranate
for the change that did not come
soon enough. Every seed a heart, every heart
a minefield, and the bees and butterflies
swarm the flowers on its grave.
The thornbushes instruct us
to tell our sons and daughters
who carry sticks and stones
to mend their ways.
The oak tree says to eat
only fruits and vegetables;
the pine says to eat all the stirring things.
My neighbor left long ago and did not hear
any of this. In a big country
the leader warns the leader of a small country
there must be change or else.
Birds are the same way, coming and going,
wobbling thin branches.
The warblers express pain, the crows regret.
Or is it the other way around?
The mantra today the same as yesterday.
We must become different.
The plants must, the animals,
and the ants and worms, just like the carmakers,

the soap makers before them,
and the manufacturers of rubber
and the sellers of tea, tobacco, and salt.
Such an ancient habit, making ourselves new.
My neighbor looks like my mother
who left a long time ago
and did not hear any of this.
Just for a minute, give her back to me,
before she died, kneeling
in the dirt under the sun, calling me darling
in Arabic, which no one has since.

NEIGHBORS

George killed men in the war.
Which men, which war, he doesn't say, and I don't ask.
The flowers in his yard, poppies or anemones,
remain the most beautiful on the street.

///

The brothers next door celebrate with shots
to the moon. Falling rain wets their foreheads,
their shingled rooftop, the tall pines rising above the chimney,
the soaring tips of their bullets.

///

The chemistry or calculus teacher, Janet or Janice,
her dog shits on my grass, she never picks up after.
The one time I said something, at the curb,
she told me her son, tall and handsome, had turned on himself.
She touched her temple. "Went this way, straight through."

///

The accountant cannot get rid of the vine
creeping and covering the shrubs alongside his house.
After the divorce he stopped on a bridge,
leaned and let the weight slip into a current
flowing fast to the Atlantic.

EMPATHY

After being with you, I saw a beetle
stuck on its back, scuttling
its legs. I could have crushed it
with my heel, but I left it alone
for the ants to devour—
the ants did not come.

TERRORISM

At a college in Dearborn,
Michigan, students listened
to me read a poem
about me at camp
watching girls
hold their breaths
under the showers
so I could see
their breasts swell.

Some people call Dearborn
a hub of "terrorist" activity.
I've placed the word terrorist
between quotation marks
because "Arab" or "Muslim"
or "people who look like
the terrorists we fear"
is what they mean.

In my poem about the camp,
"Camp Dearborn,"
I use the words *pussy*
and *chickenshit*, and place them
between quotes
but for different reasons:
in the poem, I'm waiting in line
to jump over a dam
into a river where other boys
have drowned—I hesitate
until someone shouts

"pussy" and "chickenshit"
and you don't need me
to tell you what I did,
what I had to do.

A famous poet says
for a speaker to express
authority, he must possess
three virtues,
one of which is passion.

After the reading in Dearborn,
a young man
approached me.
He turned out to be
the younger brother of someone
I knew and wrote
a poem about—a lifeguard
who saved a drowning girl.

Passion is a deep-seated conviction,
says the famous poet.
You need to believe
that I believe.

I told the young man
in Dearborn about his brother
saving a life, as if
he didn't already know.
He listened, politely,
until I stopped talking
and then said I was

out of line and had acted
inappropriately. How, I asked.
He said I shouldn't use words
like that. Which, I asked.
He was getting flustered.
I wanted him to say
"pussy" and "chickenshit."
He said I should not use words
like that in front of women.
By "women," he meant
Arab and Muslim women.
Maybe he meant
all women.

A lot of Arabs and Muslims
live in Dearborn.
Some think of it
as a hotbed of Islamic terrorism.
The phrase "a hotbed
of Islamic terrorism"
probably should appear
between quotes every time
people use it, even if they are
Arab or Muslim, like me.

The famous poet says
the other virtues
a speaker should possess
are discrimination
and inclusiveness.
By "discrimination"
he means the speaker

should come to his position
without ignoring but by considering
opposed positions
and finding them wanting.
By "inclusiveness"
he means the speaker
immediately sees connections
between the subject at hand
and other issues.
Also, the speaker needs
to make the reader believe
he is doing his subject justice,
that he is relating it
to the world,
making his voice
communal, speaking not
for any community
but with the goal of making
communities, the first of which
is that of speaker and reader.

The young man speaking
on behalf of Arab and Muslim
women told me
that my poems were "indecent"
and "immoral"—
I should be ashamed—
I was a terrible Muslim.

"Go fuck yourself"
is what I wanted to say,
but maybe he was right—
I smiled, thanked him

for listening, and told him
I loved his brother.
"Please, will you say
I said hello."

SELF-PORTRAIT AS TREES

You look yellow
like American smoke tree, sassafras, huisache,
witch hazel. What about Carolina
holly? Bebb willow? Ashe
juniper and scarlet oak? And your wife,
is she infected? You can never be sure.
When was the last time you were sugar maple,
black spruce, ginkgo, or white poplar?
You look thin. You may make it,
or not. Livers and kidneys fail, marriages
fall apart, men leave their homes, never
go back. There is a reason why:
why pollen, why bark, why spur, conifer, and pitch.
When I touch here,
can you stop shaking?
Give me your arm, your shadow
mountain ash, your devil's-walking-stick.
Let me see your eastern burning bush.
Something is still wrong. Something is tree,
leaf, flower, fruit.
How do you say your name?
It is simply not true
everyone wants to live.
Some of us want to sweet gum, some of us
want to yaupon, to sour gum.
It's not true everyone wants to live.
Some of us want to honey locust,
or hackberry or sumac.
Some of us simply do not
want to pine or willow or ash.

ON THE DEATH OF OTHER PEOPLE'S CHILDREN

Their deaths astonish
even the trees,

but in no time we live again,
the joys
they lost
and never knew.

Someone must
tell the mothers and fathers
to eat, drink, and sleep,
to sing and dance.

Someone else
must tell them
not to.

ALL THESE QUESTIONS YOU ASK

I know traps. I caught a pigeon
when I was a boy in the age
of Kodachrome. I posed with a rifle
for a black-and-white photograph.
I thought I looked like a young
Paul Newman. You were thinking
Omar Sharif, weren't you? In Syria,
Iraq, Iran, Kuwait, Egypt, and Libya,
men with smooth hands
stamped my passport, served me
mint tea, rolled cigarettes, recited
poetry, and joked about their wives,
their presidents, their Gods.
In the name of God, I have cursed a thousand times
the name of God. Once,
I paid for a prostitute. It was Amsterdam,
I was young, she taught me
not to be ashamed. I bought her
a sandwich, she read me
Hemingway. Her name,
she would not tell me her real name.
Fair enough. I told her mine
is Haboob. Do you not understand
the joke? Do you need me
to say it was terrible? Once,
I bought Broadway tickets
and walked to Canal Street
for a Rolex. Of course it was fake,
but I paid $10 and can you tell?
My brother died in a taxicab.
No one took responsibility.

My neighbor wrote a blog, wildly
popular and widely criticized—for months
no one has seen him. I don't know
what happened to everyone else.
My mother saw Nina Simone
in Antibes. She sang her to me
the day she died. Even where you live,
how popular do you really think
"Moon River" is? You can, if you wish,
easily memorize "Quds al Atiqa."
I grew vegetables on my windowsill.
I drew a map of my country
before you arrived. My wife can speak
for herself. My sons—do you see someone
behind me? Real or imagined,
my sons and daughters grow
tall as redwoods. Once, I studied the law.
My bones were always worth
as much as yours.

SELF-PORTRAIT WITH WOMAN
ON THE SUBWAY

Across from me she
was crying badly, everyone
around her looking
into their laps trying
to pretend they did not notice.
So unashamed
in her grief she wept
like the N line
was a room in her apartment
and the afternoon
would last forever.
Twenty years on,
I could've said something,
anything—
"The red of your scarf
is beautiful."

THE PROBLEM WITH ME IS THE PROBLEM
WITH YOU

A dog outside barks loudly.
Inside, everything quiet.
I said I would not, but here
I am looking:
dogs snarling and lunging at
men naked and hooded.

Animals don't know
shame, and mine I love but not
so much because love like
oil spreads thin,
clings—
to the heart, the mind,

I don't know—
and I suspect, when I leave
her for days on end, she gets
depressed.
No woman has ever
watched me close the door with

such sad eyes—yes, I've changed
the subject. Driving
to the airport I think these days
people long
for what is happening
to make sense or to make

sense of what is happening:
for example, the woman holding

the leash is smiling
while the man
attached to it tries to hide
his shame. Sometimes,

men want to be
like nature.
All around hanging, falling, falling
to pieces
the leaves of oak, pine, maple,
magnolia, and cypress—

too many to count.
There will be leaves
to bag when I return home, and,
yes, men in foreign lands will be
sent home,
and for each his own means

of delivery—a seat,
a plastic bag.
Days like today, times
like these, I don't want
a damn thing
to do with victims.

In the terminal, through
the windows, the twilight almost
imperceptible, evening
coming on quickly, and the color
of the sky I don't
notice. Waiting, I look

around—nothing here
compares to anything
there. I may look
like them, these men who grew
old by torture,
but I am not.

On the long flight I take
the aisle for comfort
and the illusion
of safety, and I leave
the view to the woman
beside me watching

me—
she looks like
someone I would make
small talk for, buy
a drink—
I speak kindly, an act

like the weather, as much prophecy
as science, and like
the weather what makes me
frightening—
terror in her heart,
her mind—

is invisible, capable
of being
identified or anticipated only

by those in the know.
She has big brown eyes
and I believe that

she believes
at my mercy she will thrive
or perish.
I reduce myself
to clichés: when she says nothing
at all, I talk

about the weather.
I think
she is an expert of sorts:
everyone knows something
about someone.
And the wise

interpret for those
who cannot read the signs:
turbulence ahead, trouble to come,
and on every horizon,
a disappearance.

UNRESOLVED HAIKU

UNRESOLVED

When he is with her,
some nights, he feels like a fish
in a frying pan.

Then there are the times
when he'd rather burn to death
than be without her.

BEAUTIFUL MORNING

The lizard sunning
outside the house, the cat wants
to kill so badly.

BEING A MOTHER AND FATHER

Sometimes love means not
throwing a wailing infant
through a windowpane.

GETTING BY

Wedged behind the door,
a shovel to keep thieves out—
twice still they broke through.

HOW IT HAPPENED

Little by little
and then all of a sudden,
the marriage collapsed.

OLD COUPLE

Whoever wakes first
checks to see if the other
made it through the night.

SUMMERTIME

Where the children play,
fire ant mounds like land mines
wait for their footsteps.

SEEING OUR MOTHER YEARS AFTER
SHE DIED

Hallucination,
I say. You, ghost. Either way,
she's not coming back.

CONDOLENCE THEN APOLOGY

For the stillborn child,
and for feeling glad that you,
not me, suffered this.

HIGH SCHOOL ANGST,
HIGH SCHOOL TRYST

Turns out it mattered
not at all that you could not
dance to save your life.

THE RIVER IN WINTER

Cold, clear, no hint yet
of the summer tourists or
their empty beer cans.

WHAT DOESN'T KILL YOU
MAKES YOU STRONGER

Was one of the things
people said to him, and her,
to comfort, to ease.

Her death went slowly.
The picture of good health, he
joined her by the spring.

PRELUDE

And the Flood was forty days over the earth. . . . And the waters surged
most mightily over the earth. . . . And all flesh that stirs on the earth
perished, the fowl and the cattle and the beasts and all swarming things
that swarm upon the earth, and all humankind. All that had the quickening
breath of life in its nostrils, of all that was on dry land, died. . . .
He wiped out all existing things from the face of the earth,
from humans to cattle to crawling things to the fowl of the heavens,
everything wiped from the earth.

///

Rage—

What god drove them to fight with such a fury?

But one man, Thersites, still railed on, nonstop.
His head full of obscenities, teeming with rant,
all for no good reason insubordinate, baiting the kings. . . .
Here was the ugliest man who ever came to Troy.
Bandy-legged he was, with one foot clubbed,
both shoulders humped together, curving over
his caved-in chest, and bobbing above them
his skull warped to a point,
sprouting clumps of scraggly, woolly hair.
Achilles despised him most, Odysseus too. . . .

But Odysseus stepped in quickly, faced him down
with a dark glance and threats to break his nerve:

"Keep quiet. . . .
Stop your babbling. . . .

You and your ranting slander—*you're* the outrage.
I tell you this, so help me it's the truth:
if I catch you again, blithering on this way . . .
if I don't grab you, strip the clothing off you,
cloak, tunic and rags that wrap your private parts,
and whip you howling naked . . ."

And he cracked the scepter across his back and shoulders.
The rascal doubled over, tears streaking his face
and a bloody welt bulged up between his blades. . . .
He squatted low, cringing, stunned with pain,
blinking like some idiot . . .
rubbing his tears off dumbly with a fist.
Their morale was low but the men laughed now,
good hearty laughter breaking over Thersites' head."

///

I sing of warfare and a man at war.

                    As Tarquitus
vainly pled, and would have pled again,
the Trojan struck his head off to the ground,
then with his foot made the warm trunk roll over,
speaking above him from his pitiless heart:
"Lie there now, fearsome as you are. No gentle
mother will ever hide you in the earth
or weight your body with a family tomb.
Either you stay here for the carrion birds
or the sea takes you under, hungry fishes
nibble your wounds."

And deaths like these all over the battlefield
the Dardan captain brought about, in fury
wild as a torrent or a dark tornado.

FUGUE

Life is a game, the first rule of which is that it is not a game.
It is deadly serious.

Nothing more obvious than what our politicians do to our language, so if we
insist on the truth, on an accurate rendition, a faithful use of language, if we insist
on an accurate depiction of people's lives as they actually live them—this becomes
a political act.

When we played, it was always war. In our hands, any old stick was a weapon,
pine cones were bombs. "If everyone plays war," said my mother, "there will be war."
She was right—there was.

///

True creation is always purposeless, without ulterior motive.

Your whole notion of reality is just a lie. Your country
isn't what you had been told it was, the others aren't what
you'd been told they were. Nobody is what you'd been told
they were. The past is utter horseshit.

In the beginning was the bomb.

///

Trying to scratch the itch makes the itch worse, but an itch wants to be scratched.
When it's clear beyond all doubt that the itch cannot be scratched, it stops itching
by itself. When we realize that our basic desire is a vicious cycle, it stops circling
of its own accord. There is no way of *making* it stop.

I pick up a book and say, "Uh-uh, New York," dismissing it without coping with what it might be saying. I can pick up the goddamn book and say, "Uh-uh, Iowa," "Ah, Beat, hip, Black Mountain . . ." and slip it in a pigeonhole. It's a waste of time. But if I pick up one of those books, read it, and say, "My heavens, this guy is doing things I never thought of doing, he's talking about the stars, flowers, his neighbor," then I might suddenly be shocked into my deadness to my neighbors, flowers, and the stars. I might learn something. I might become a different kind of poet.

The most important thing is to avoid panic. It is not the dead who are in danger of succumbing to the demands of the attacker. It is the terrified.

///

If you look at Jan van Eyck's painting of the Last Judgment, everybody in heaven is completely bored—sitting there looking like the cat that swallowed the canary. Rows and rows of them with the Lord God Almighty presiding and looking equally bored. All those stately people in heaven are destined to stay in church forever, in an obvious state of ultimate boredom. But down below there is a bat-winged skull spreading out its ghastly wings, and all-nude bodies writhing, being eaten by snakes and each other—an orgy. We have never admitted that our idea of heaven is a perfectly useless state.

The other day I was sitting on the train with a young woman and she began talking about mime, about these problems she would work on, all very vague at first, so I said, "What the hell is a real problem, tell me one." She said, "Looking someone in the eyes." It was startling. So much of being a poet is looking other people in the eyes. Looking yourself in the eyes. Accepting vulnerability.

It's better that women and children die than they become hysterical and create panic. Bang, you're dead. It's for the best.

///

But now, here is the thing that I am getting at:
a culture that excludes frivolity has lost the point of life.

A political poet doesn't necessarily tell people
how to vote, how to think, or what specific attitudes
they should have, but deals with the political facts of our lives—
that we live at the pleasure of people with enormous power
and very little compassion, that there is very little justice
in the world, that most of what young people are told,
and older for that matter, about the nature of this country,
this America, is nonsense.

It is primarily men who are entertained. For them, war is
temptation, pleasure, and proof of their masculinity.
Should they ever be faced with such a choice, men might
very well give up women before they give up war.

///

For growth to happen, first, you must have the technical ability
to express what happens. Second, you must get out of your own way.

Abstract ideas are so monumental all the way from Plato to the present.
They bore me. Philosophers bore me. I find them the most boring people
I've ever come across in my life. I'd much prefer spending an afternoon
with a bunch of jockeys or car mechanics than with philosophers.
I remember renting my house to a philosopher who let all the trees die.
And when I got angry with him, because my wife planted those trees
and loved them—seven trees he let die—he said, "I didn't think you were
the kind of man who would care about something like that." That was
the voice of the philosopher, "something like that"—a living thing.

When may one wage war? What's permissible in war? Depends
on who the enemy is. The laws of war protect enemies of the same race,
class, and culture. The laws of war leave the foreign and the alien
without protection. When is one allowed to wage war against savages
and barbarians? Answer: always. What is permissible in wars against
savages and barbarians? Answer: anything.

/ / /

The ego "sees" sights, "hears" sounds, "feels" feelings, and "has" experiences.
These are common but redundant ways of talking, for seeing a sight is just seeing,
hearing a sound is just hearing, feeling a feeling is just feeling, and having
an experience is just experiencing. But that these redundant phrases are so
commonly used shows that most people think of themselves as separate
from their thoughts and experiences.

You said John Berryman taught you a lot about poetry and its importance.
How did he think poetry was important? He was able to pick up the newspaper,
full of Eisenhower, John Foster Dulles, Joe McCarthy and the various
American idiots of the time, and he'd say, "Kids, this will pass. These idiots
will be replaced by other idiots. Don't worry about it." Then he'd put alongside
that paper the poems of John Keats and say, "This will not pass as long as
our language is spoken. Some things are transient and some things
come close to being permanent. Don't lose sight of that."

And yet from the beginning, genocide is inscribed in our earliest and holiest texts.
The Old Testament, *The Iliad*, *The Aeneid*. There are your instructions.

/ / /

We are not victims of a conspiracy arranged by an external God
or some secret society of manipulators. If there is any biological
foundation for the hoax, it lies only in the brain's capacity

for narrowed, attentive consciousness hand in hand with its power
of recognition—of knowing about knowing and thinking about thinking
with the use of images and language. My problem as a writer,
using words, is to dispel the illusions of language while employing
one of the languages that generates them. I can succeed only
on the principle of a hair of the dog that bit you.

I don't want to be close to the centers of literary power and be
influenced by them. It's very dangerous. You can fool
yourself into thinking that because people come to your readings
or buy your books that you're really a terrific poet.

You will probably go through several emotional reactions
when you kill. These are generally sequential but not necessarily
universal. The first phase is concern that you'll freeze up
and won't be able to pull the trigger. The second is the actual kill,
which, because of your training, will happen reflexively.
You may feel exhilarated. Killing produces adrenaline;
repeated killing can lead to a "killing addiction." This feeling
can be especially intense if you kill at medium to long-range distances.
The next phase, remorse and revulsion, can render you unable
to ever kill again. Dave Grossman presents this "collage of pain
and horror": "my experience was one of revulsion and disgust . . .
I dropped my weapon and cried . . . there was so much blood . . .
I vomited . . . and I cried . . . I felt remorse and shame. . .
I can remember whispering foolishly, 'I'm sorry' and then
just throwing up." Only a few people are able to kill
and not feel remorse, though many try to deny this feeling
to make it easier to continue to kill. Subsequent killings are often
easier to handle. Last is the rationalization and acceptance phase,
a lifelong process during which you will try to account for

what you did. Most are able to see what they did as the right
and necessary thing. If you cannot rationalize your killing,
it may lead to post-traumatic stress disorder.

///

The startling truth is that our best efforts for civil rights,
international peace, population control, conservation
of natural resources, and assistance to the starving of the earth—
urgent as they are—will destroy rather than help if made
in the present spirit. For, as things stand, we have nothing
to give. If our own riches and our own way of life are not
enjoyed here, they will not be enjoyed elsewhere. Peace
can be made only by those who are peaceful, and love
can be shown only by those who love. No work of love
will flourish out of guilt, fear, or hollowness of heart,
just as no valid plans for the future can be made by those
who have no capacity for living now.

Good poems demand to be written from inside the poet.
What happens with most political poems is that poets
in certain situations think a poem is needed, and they
are obliged to sit down and write it, producing crap.

One very important way in which men can attain joy, freedom,
happiness, even delirium and ecstasy, is by not staying home
with wife and family, even to the point where, often enough,
they are only too happy to give up their nearest and dearest
in favor of—war!

///

The more resolutely you plumb the question "Who or what am I?"—
the more unavoidable the realization that you are nothing at all
apart from everything *else*. Yet again, the more you strive for some
kind of perfection or mastery—in morals, art, or spirituality—
the more you see that you are playing a rarefied and lofty form of
the old ego-game, and that your attainment of any height is apparent
to yourself and to others only by contrast with someone else's depth
or failure.

Most of what we're taught is simply illusion. I start school when
I'm five, and what's the first thing I'm taught? I am important,
I'm a citizen of the United States, I could be president because
this is like no other country. Well, first I couldn't be president
for twenty reasons. Then this country is like the others.
And finally the United States is an illusion.

We burn their villages, we cut down their fruit trees, we massacre
their women and children. Is this, I ask you, the best way
to teach them to love civilization?

///

The sense of paralysis is therefore the dawning realization
that this is nonsense and that your independent ego is
a fiction. It simply isn't there, either to do anything or
to be pushed around by external forces, to change things
or to submit to change. The sense of "I," which should
have been identified with the whole universe of your experience,
was instead cut off, isolated as a detached observer of that universe.

Does this mean you have trouble being a good citizen? No.
I'm a good citizen.

Better to die than to allow my fear to infect those who had
to be heroes. It was a foregone conclusion. I agreed with it.
I even liked it. It gave me a sense of sacrifice and dignity
that was exuberantly matter of course. You got me, I'm dead.

/ / /

To paraphrase the Gospel: love your competitors, and pray for those who
undercut your prices. The political and personal morality of the West,
especially in the United States, is—for lack of this sense—utterly schizophrenic.
It is a monstrous combination of uncompromising idealism and unscrupulous
gangsterism, and thus devoid of the humor and humaneness which enables
confessed rascals to sit down together and work out reasonable deals.
No one can be moral—no one can harmonize contained conflicts—without
coming to a working arrangement between his rose above and his manure below.

One of the most attractive qualities about a poem is its ambition.

"Bang, you're dead," we said. "Now you're dead," we said.

// // //

SELF-PORTRAIT AFTER A FUNERAL

I bought groceries, washed
dishes, peeled
oranges for the kids, watched
TV—all the while and into the night

I had profound thoughts.
And by the morning I knew
for sure
they were not.

BEES, HONEYCOMBS, HONEY

Bees, thousands and thousands,
surviving in a hive
under the soffit; bees,
honeycombs, and honey,
and dampness, and old wood
sticky in the sunlight;

and the beekeeper's hand,
carefully, and slowly,
vacuuming, and taking;
the bees tumbling gently
into the makeshift hive;
honeybees, and honeycombs,

and honey, glistening;
honey, the only food
that will not spoil; honey,
pulled from the pyramids,
still sticky and sweet,
thousands of years later;

I may not believe, but
I want to; and the bees
before my eyes are now
disappearing; bees God
in the Qur'an inspired
to build homes in mountains

and trees; bees that built homes
in the trees near the grave
in Detroit; and the bees

in Jerusalem's graves;
bees in every city,
and in every age; bees,

honey, and honeycombs,
through disaster after
disaster; bees building,
and scouting, and dancing;
bees mating, protecting,
and attacking; the bees

are now disappearing,
and dying; and the bees
the beekeeper cannot
save are dying but still
guarding the empty hive,
butting their heads against

the children, who will grow
into men and women,
and build homes, now dipping
fingers into honey
darkening on the ground;
they are dying; the hive

is gone; the queen is gone;
thousands and thousands, gone;
but the bees will come back,
and the hive will come back;
if not here, then elsewhere;
and there will be more bees

making more honeycombs,
more honey, and more bees;
and one day all the bees
will be gone; gone, and gone;
honeycombs, and houses,
gone; and trees, gone; oak, elm,

birch, gone; all trees, flowers,
gone; and birds, leaves, branches,
cicadas, and crickets,
grasshoppers, ants, worms, gone;
and cities, and rivers,
big cities, small cities,

big rivers, small rivers,
gardens, and homes; and homes;
the bees will be gone, and
only their honey will
survive, and we will not
be around to taste it.

THE SYMBOLIC LIFE

They kept showing up for days
dead on the windowsill,
and for days I did nothing about the ladybugs
except to ask if their entering the house
unnoticed and dying before I saw them
was symbolic.
Thinking so was easy.
They symbolized birth and death,
change and rebirth.
It was also possible the tiny beetles
embodied an inborn need
to show themselves,
to turn up in every and any place,
even as the dried out remains of the once lively.
Or they stood for the burden of being one thing
relieved by becoming another,
which all the world's children suffer.
This went on and on, and could've gone on
forever, so finally I opened the window
and blew them into the wide open
because everything and everyone should get a chance
to be mourned, and they got theirs,
but first they had to die, which is life,
not symbolism.

SELF-PORTRAIT AS SCIENTIFIC
OBSERVATION

More than anything
I wanted a girl
whose name I can't
remember now.
She was my lab partner,
and another guy in class
wanted her, too.
Every time she stepped away
he told me what he wanted
to do to her.
Every time, the same thing,
only the place changed—
"Fuck her."
Fuck her in the bathroom,
fuck her
in the library, the bookstore, the cafeteria.
"Shit, I'd fuck her
right here, on this spot."
I looked at the lab's cold, hard floor.
"Really?"
"Fuck yeah."
Week after week he kept at it,
and I only laughed off
his fantasies,
which became more boring
than chemistry itself.
Eventually, I got up the nerve
to ask her out.
She said no quickly.
I gave up easily.

"Fucking cunt,"
he called her.
She went on to medical school.
I imagine she's done well.
Last year, I failed
to describe
a spider. I imagine
she never thinks of me at all.

THE DAY PHIL LEVINE DIED

My father never asked me
why I gave up
becoming a doctor
to be a poet.

I would've told him
because of a poem
by Levine
about a boy and girl

on Belle Isle
taking off their clothes
and walking
hand in hand

into the filthiest river
I knew, the Detroit River.
The poem
was beautiful,

but I kept my mouth shut
about it and Levine,
sure he'd only ask
if the poet

was a Jew.
He only ever talked
to one Jew,
the owner of a furniture shop

by the Rouge,
and only to haggle
over the price
of a sofa or dining set

he wasn't planning
to buy.
He could've said a lot
that I might have

listened to:
poems won't pay bills,
and the companies hiring
don't give a shit

about all the poems
written in English,
or Arabic,
or any language.

He'd never read
a poem of mine,
and didn't bother
to ask if anyone

in the world thought
they were any good.
He might've
pointed out how poor

and destitute
so many poets died.
But he did none of this.
I told him

I was going to be a poet,
regardless of failure,
and he put a gun to my head
and said, "No."

THE PRIZE

A book with poems
about Bessie Smith,
Marilyn Monroe,
Queen Elizabeth,
William Tell,
W. B. Yeats,
Ted Hughes,
Sitting Bull,
an otter, a fox, and a hare
won the Pulitzer Prize
in the first year
of the war.

In the second year,
the year of insurgency,
of bridges, corpses,
blindfolds, and dogs,
a poet who wrote
about the only species
that commits suicide
received the prize.

In the year of boycotts
and stained fingertips,
the third of the war,
the prize went
to a retired life insurance executive
who lived on acreage
near the village of Garland,
Nebraska.

Disappearance,
from one life
to another,
was the subject
of the prizewinner
in the year of growing
sectarian violence,
the fourth of the war,
also the year of verdict
and hanging.

In the fifth year,
of surge
and black water,
the civil war continued,
and the prize
was given to a book
about our civil war,
which ended
143 years earlier.

In the sixth year,
the prize was granted
to a poet who wrote a lovely poem
about war, the war
in Europe,
where white men
killed each other
by the millions;
his poem
still mentioned an Arab,
a young man who performs
an act of purification,

removing hair
from his body,
before flying
a plane into an office building,
an act that took place
fifty-eight years after the war
the poem is actually about.

The prize was shared
in the sixth year of the war,
the other book
evoking pleasures
(of family, beaches, and dogs)
and horrors
(of young men
purifying their bodies
with speed
and conviction).

In the seventh year,
the year of ceasefire
and effigy,
the prize was presented
to a book about loss,
memory,
and the continuum of time;
the book was named
after a dog
in the sky.

The war went on,
for eight years now,
and many

soldiers
(three hundred thousand)
were returned home,
and many
others
(not soldiers,
too many to count)
were returned
to the earth;
this was the year
of exit strategies,
and a book described as filled
with "little thought bombs"
won the Pulitzer Prize.

In the year of renaming,
the ninth, a new dawn
replaced freedom,
and the prize winner
had served
as United States Poet Laureate
in the war's sixth,
seventh, and eighth years.

The last year,
the year of withdrawal,
the prize was given to a book
named after life
on another planet,
which is a yearning
for another way to live,
which is also
another way to die.

Long after life on Earth
the depleted uranium
in the Tigris
will reach its half-life,
four and a half billion years
after the tenth year of the war,
which is
the end of time.

MEAN

SIBLING RIVALRY

When he hit her,
I laughed.
I could not
stop laughing.
Then he belted
me for cracking
up over her
punishment, and I
heard her burst
into hysterics.

AT THE PARTY

Talking to the woman
with the shaved head
dying of a disease I didn't ask
the name of,
I didn't pretend everything
would turn out fine
or tell her to call on me
anytime, for anything.

I sat there nodding
while she talked, talked, talked,
and cried.
She didn't look half bad
for someone who'd be dead
in less than a month.

TO THE POET

who lost her home to a hurricane
and suffered an asthma attack
during the cigarette break I took
and told me, "It's not
that I don't like you—

I don't like people"—
and whose sociopathic tendencies
worsened on account of things I said
and who regularly accused me of stealing
the little joy she received from life:

you broke my heart.
And I thanked the sun, stars, and moon
when you got sick
and did not come back.

SELF-PORTRAIT WITH EMPTY PACK
OF CIGARETTES

I stopped smoking
because someone I knew
died of emphysema,

and I sincerely wanted
to die of something
much better than that.

ACROSS THE COUNTRY FROM A
CEMETERY IN MICHIGAN

On the corner I saw a woman
without teeth
begging.
I thought of my mother,
who looked beautiful
the day she died,
and then I felt
much better.

SINCERITY

I watched a spider go under
my child's bed. There,
found a web strewn with white sacs.
Spiders are beautiful, I told my child,
their webs astonishing.
When she fell asleep,
I crushed them all with a book.

SUDDENLY AND UNEXPECTEDLY AND
FROM NO CLEARLY UNDERSTOOD CAUSE

I watched a dog this morning
cross the freeway easily

making its way
to the end of the world.

SELF-PORTRAIT WITH CURSES AT 35,000 FEET

On a flight to Detroit
the guy next to me
told me
about his shitty job,
his dumb,
slobbering dog,
his good-for-nothing
kids, two of them—
assholes—and his lying,
cheating wife.
Moving
at 500 mph
above the earth without
feeling it,
I listened to him go on
and on, his pain
bad to worse—

to what wisdom
does suffering
give birth?
—and must we always
learn from it?
Earlier
that morning,
my mother had died,
and going back to her,
once
and for all,
I would find out.

But first
I had to suffer
Bob—
fucking Bob.

MICHIGAN

Near a lake where no one fished
he stood the way three hundred years before
a Frenchman would have,
hand on hip, the other wiping
a sweaty brow, and he squinted
far off into the horizon
where birch and maple topped a hill,

licked his thumb, held it
to a breeze burning with hairspray,
and to my astonishment
guessed the hour and minute exactly.

Years later, the middle of winter,
I went back. The lake, man-made,
had been drained. The trees,
sickly pine. And on a rise,
hardly a hill, I saw what before
I had been too small to see back then,
too young to realize: a clock tower.

With time, I overcame
my disappointment. I became
like him, with children
of my own to amaze
and ruin.

THE NIGHT THE DOG DIED

When the dog yelped
and tottered across the yard,
tree to tree stump
to grass patch, stopping once
to sniff the air and then,
knowing or not, lay down
to die, I heard the neighbors
through their walls
fighting again.
The moon full,
the sky clear.

SELF-PORTRAIT WITH DOG, POSSUM,
NEWSPAPER, AND SHOVEL

From the fence and from the possum
with the deep gash across its neck, I drag the dog.
And when, the temperature

steadily climbing, I come back close enough
to see its punctured left eye and broken back,
the possum hisses.

The dog did this as a game
or else being what she is, a thing
of unthinking and sometimes violent force,

which is right for a dog.
I hear her now, tied up
behind me, growling, snarling, whimpering

for the kill, and over the possum's head
I lay the newspaper with its everyday, everywhere
reminders of always something—

a blindfold cinched, a bomb
among tomatoes and cucumbers, another animal
forever passing through our lives—

raising the shovel high
I think this is right
but also hard.

The first blow is not enough,
and I come down again,
harder.

THE OTHER WOMAN

My wife dreamed
I fucked her friend from college,
a blonde with a better body,
better job, who told funnier jokes
and read Nietzsche.

I had never met my wife's friend
and in the dream
she only vaguely resembled anyone
my wife actually knew.

For three days, still,
she ignored my phone calls,
slept with her back turned to me,
pouring salt on the leftovers
I'd saved for lunch.

SELF-PORTRAIT WITH CASSETTE PLAYER

Before going into the bar,
I used to sit in my car listening
to Bach for twenty,
thirty, forty, fifty,
sixty minutes, sometimes more,
sometimes Beethoven
or Mendelssohn, Chopin or Schubert.
So long as the sound
was not another person
talking about something I didn't care about,
I didn't care
whose music it was.
I could wait in the lot a long time.
Far be it from me to tell others
half of anything they ever said
meant nothing
before they ever said it.
So much happening
was impossible: people
who looked like me murdering
people who looked like me.
All the same, for thousands
of years it had happened
thousands of times, which is why
some nights I left the bar drunk
and some I never left
the car at all.

PERSONAL POLITICAL POEM

Around midnight I stalled
outside a police station
in Henry Ford's hometown.
The cops told me to keep
walking. A mile later

the Arab gas station attendant—
the name embroidered on his shirt
said Sam—he talked
and talked and talked.
He asked if I recognized him.

He said when we were young
we knew each other.
He'd been to the house
I grew up in. His father
loved my father, his mother

loved my mother.
He said he was sorry
for what happened.
He said we're all dying,
but we should get to grow old

and *just like that* shouldn't be
how a life ends. He said
he was at the funeral.
Seeing me carry the casket
made him imagine

one day doing the same.
I said it was late, I needed
to get back, the cops
were going to tow my car.
He showed me a newspaper.

He said he was the guy
who pulled a drowning girl
from a crowded pool.
He pointed to the mayor
shaking his hand. He said

he went to high school with the mayor
who was the kind of guy
who would jab his finger
at your chest and say,
"You don't look like a Sam."

There was something better
out there, he said. He knew
there was. For him. For me.
I told him it was true
he did not look like a Sam.

NOTHING HAPPENED IN 1999

A king did not die, a president
was not acquitted, a balloon
did not fly around the world
in twenty days. At eighty-four,
with white hair, Joe DiMaggio
was not mourned. And air strikes
launched street to street
in order to bring peace,
or a doctor convicted of doctoring
death? No, and no. Nothing
happened, except flowers purple
the year before bloomed
white, but no viruses named
after women spread across
the globe, and the word
"columbine" did not enter
the consciousness of a nation.
What about the bomb
that made a mistake, or the famous
son of a famous president
mistaking the ocean for the sky?
That year, the weather was
unpredictable, that happened,
and if anything else did,
like shots fired at people
praying, no one heard them,
and if people prayed for war
to become holy, those prayers
went unanswered. In Turkey,
the ground split open and
the seventeen thousand who would die, let's say,

miraculously, they did not, not
in 1999, the year two lifelong
enemies shook hands and said
there will be peace, but
their palms never touched, why
lie about that? Let's say
the child from Cuba arrived
not an orphan but with his mother,
who loved and did not sink into
the sea. Let's not talk
about rampages, disasters,
conflicts, or coups that never
ruined a perfectly good year
during which the sun shined
on the moon, the earth,
and six billion who, for once,
got everything right
and not a single thing wrong.

THAT SUMMER THAT YEAR DURING
THE HEAT WAVE

What did we think sitting there
on the front porch, without fear, none at all,
no surprise or shock,
barefoot, slow breathing, the sun

unyielding even under elm and maple,
thirty-five years ago,
I wasn't yet twelve, my sister not ten, the city
months from the riots after the World Series?

Two men ran down the middle of the street,
the one in front yelling
(how far he made it—
the ice cream parlor, the diner, the liquor store, the bowling alley—

I can't say), and the other one,
chasing after him, aiming a shotgun, he looked at us,
smiled, and I saw
all his teeth.

1979

We were stopped
at a red light, I was in the passenger seat,
and a guy crossing the street looked
at the Buick, then at us, flipped
us the middle finger and said,
"Go home, camel jockeys."
However hard I try, I can't remember
if, then and there, what the guy said
made any difference to me.
I was seven—what did I know
about crisis? As for the guy,
before the light turned green,
my father floored the pedal
and ran him over.

ODE ON AN ABANDONED HOUSE

Wind and rain, here
are the keys
to the house—
a missing door,
two broken windows.

Birds, for you a room
with a view—the bedroom,
which once held
the moon and stars
out of sight.

Ants and worms,
such sad witnesses,
the grass uncut
and the yard overgrown
are again yours to inherit.

And you, the leaves whirling
across buckled floors,
please take
my father's voice
whispering

May you live forever,
may you bury me.

APOKALUPTEIN

١

The Arab apocalypse began around the year
of my birth, give or take—
the human apocalypse,
a few thousand years earlier.

٢

I earn my living
teaching about the human condition, a composite
of violence, vengeance, and theft,
ingenuity, too, and forms of love unique
to men and women, the only species
that knows, consciously, what others of its kind
thought and did thousands of years before—
stories, myths, histories, philosophies,
all mirrors and constellations
showing humanity to itself,
none of which
will ensure our survival.

٣

A mile, a mile and a half from the border,
the Israeli border, Bint Jbeil,
the small city my father left
in 1967,
its orchards, hillsides, rivers,
roads, highways, bridges,
houses, schools, restaurants, coffee shops,
pharmacies, hospitals, cemeteries,
twice in his lifetime, obliterated.

ء

The Arab apocalypse began in the 1950s and '60s,
in Egypt, Tunisia, Libya, Syria, and Iraq—
the human apocalypse,
in 1945, in a desert in New Mexico
where scientists exploded the first atomic bomb.

ه

In Beirut, snipers picked off children sneaking
to buy candy, yet the population grew.

٦

In 1972 my father paid $9,000
for a house in Detroit.
Forty years later, a foreclosure, it sold for $8,000,
its windows, doors, floors, walls,
the porch, the mailbox,
the tree in front, birch or poplar,
gone—now
weeds and bushes block the drive,
vines where the chimney once was
creep over the rooftop.

٧

"In free fall," an expert in urban decline
describes Detroit's population.
At the current rate, by the beginning of the next century,
stray dogs will outnumber people.

٨

Soon as I earned enough to get out, I got out.
Still a street comes to mind:
Forest, Grand, St. Aubin, Lafayette,

or the bridge over the river
to Belle Isle, or the tunnel lights
before Joe Louis Arena,
or, disappearing
in a rearview mirror, the horizon
with smokestacks, which once
upon a time I believed no other on earth
could match in perfection.

٩

The Arab apocalypse began on a piece of paper
in 1917—
the human apocalypse,
50,000 years ago,
when hunters wiped out
the giant kangaroo.

١٠

In politics, practically nothing is new.
Twenty-four hundred years ago
Plato worried about speech-acts,
what he called "craft,"
the crowd swayed so easily
by emotion and flattery, interest and advantage,
the logical failures to follow.

١١

Today, which poems will cause institutions to fail?
Who worries about that?

١٢

The city was here when lust lured us
away from the animals,

when kings and the children of gods hunted
side by side in the forests of lesser gods,
when Priam begged for his boy's broken body,
when Achilles, cruel and beautiful,
chose death for glory, when Abram became
Abraham, and Muhammad
heard God's voice in a lightning bolt—
it was here,
and the asphalt and concrete
won't reveal what it was, the rivers
won't either, or the trees or the soot turning
factory walls and lungs permanently black—
whatever it was,
swamp, forest, glacier,
it was there.

١٣

The apocalypse began
with a thousand hoofbeats
across a field, men
hollering, women wondering
where to hide
the children. "Here,"
a mother said.
"We will hide in the earth—
our ancestors are already there,
the rest will follow."

NOTES

"Under the Sun": The final lines echo phrases in Mary Oliver's "Everything."

"Porch Haiku" and "Ode on an Abandoned House" came about through a collaboration, called The Balakonah Project, with poet and photographer Marwa Helal. Envisioned by Helal, The Balakonah Project paired poetry with photographs representing Arab porch culture in Detroit and Brooklyn and was presented at the Poetry Project at St. Mark's Church in New York City, on June 19, 2019.

"Terrorism": The "famous poet" is Carl Dennis; the poetic arguments referred to are found in his essay "The Voice of Authority," from *Poetry as Persuasion* (2001).

"On the Death of Other People's Children" is in memory of Valetta Rose Kroeger.

"What Doesn't Kill You Makes You Stronger": A common adaptation of Friedrich Nietzsche's maxim "Was mich nicht umbringt, macht mich starker," from *Twilight of the Idols* (1888).

"Prelude" both quotes and paraphrases passages from the following works: Genesis, translated by Robert Alter; *The Iliad* by Homer, translated by Robert Fagles; and *The Aeneid* by Virgil, translated by Robert Fagles.

The second section brings together excerpts from the first two books of Homer's *Iliad*. Fittingly, "Rage" (*mênis* in Greek) begins the epic. Philip Metres has noted that Thersites is "the only voice in *The Iliad* to rail against the abuses of the war."

Thersites's dissent is immediately shut down by Odysseus, who is also known by the epithet "destroyer of cities."

The final section is composed of the opening line from Virgil's *Aeneid*, as well as a battle scene featuring Aeneas, the eponymous hero.

"Fugue" is comprised of interweaving quotes, at times slightly modified, from the following sources: *The Book: On the Taboo Against Knowing Who You Are* and *The Way of Liberation: Essays and Lectures on the Transformation of the Self*, both by Alan Watts; *Don't Ask*, a collection of interviews with Philip Levine; and Sven Lindqvist's *A History of Bombing*. "Fugue" also contains a single excerpt from *What Every Person Should Know About War*, by Chris Hedges.

The word *fugue* has two distinct senses, the first grounded in music, the second in psychiatry: 1. "A polyphonic composition constructed on one or more short subjects or themes, which are harmonized according to the laws of counterpoint, and introduced from time to time with various contrapuntal devices" (*Stainer and Barrett's Dictionary of Musical Terms*, by John Stainer and William Barrett). 2. "A flight from one's own identity, often involving travel to some unconsciously desired locality" (*The Oxford English Dictionary*).

"Suddenly and Unexpectedly and from No Clearly Understood Cause": The title comes from a passage in *This Is It* by Alan Watts: "The most impressive fact in man's spiritual, intellectual, and poetic experience has always been, for me, the universal prevalence of those astonishing moments of insight. . . . From all historical times and cultures we have reports of this same unmistakable sensation emerging, as a rule, quite suddenly and unexpectedly and from no clearly understood cause. To the individual thus enlightened it appears as a vivid and overwhelming certainty that the universe, precisely as it is at this moment, as a whole and in every one of its parts, is so completely *right* as to need no explanation or justification beyond what it simply is."

// // //

Every book owes something of itself to someone other than its author. Fady Joudah, Ito Romo, and Russel Swensen—thank you, for your insights, wisdom, and friendship.

ACKNOWLEDGMENTS

Thanks to the editors of the following publications, where these poems first appeared, sometimes under different titles and in their original form.

Adroit Journal: "Apokaluptein"

Cordite Review: "Porch Haiku"

Fifth Wednesday Journal: "Michigan"

Four Way Review: "Empathy"

Massachusetts Review: "Self-Portrait as Trees"

Miracle Monacle: "Some Sentences," "The Day Phil Levine Died"

Mizna: "Self-Portrait in Retrospect," "Self-Portrait with Cassette Player," "Unresolved Haiku" ("Unresolved," "Beautiful Morning," "Being a Mother and Father," "Getting By," "How It Happened," "Old Couple," "Summertime," "Seeing Our Mother Years After She Died," "Condolence Then Apology," "High School Angst, High School Tryst," "The River in Winter," "What Doesn't Kill You Makes You Stronger")

Normal School: "1979"

North American Review: "Self-Portrait as Scientific Observation," "Self-Portrait with Curses at 35,000 Feet," "The Night the Dog Died," "The Other Woman,"

Poetry: "Terrorism," "The Prize"

Poetry Now: "Nothing Happened in 1999"

Prairie Schooner: "Bees, Honeycombs, Honey"

The Recluse: "Neighbors," "Older," "That Summer That Year during the Heat Wave"

The Rumpus: "The Problem with Me Is the Problem with You"

Texas Review: "Mean" ("Sibling Rivalry," "At the Party," "To the Poet," "Self-Portrait with Empty Pack of Cigarettes,"

"Sincerity," "Suddenly and Unexpectedly and from No
Clearly Understood Cause")

upstreet: "Self-Portrait with Woman on the Subway"

Under a Warm Green Linden: "Self-Portrait after a Funeral,"
"Under the Sun"

West Branch: "All These Questions You Ask," "Personal
Political Poem," "Self-Portrait with Dog, Possum,
Newspaper, and Shovel"

// // //

"1979" and "All These Questions You Ask" also appeared in the
anthology series *Big A Little a,* edited by Clay Hunt.

"Apokaluptein" was selected for inclusion in the 2018 *Best of the
Net Anthology.*

"Elegy with Apples, Pomegranates, Bees, Butterflies,
Thornbushes, Oak, Pine, Warblers, Crows, Ants, and Worms"
was selected for inclusion in *Bettering American Poetry Volume
1* (BlazeVox Books, edited by Amy King, David Tomas
Martinez, and Sarah Clark). The poem also appeared in the
Academy of American Poets Poem-a-Day series on May 20,
2015, and in *Kyoto Journal* (Japan).

"Ode on an Abandoned House" appeared in the Poem-a-Day
series, on January 25, 2021.

"On the Death of Other People's Children" is included in
Making Mirrors: Writing/Righting by and for Refugees, edited
by Jehan Bseiso and Becky Thompson.

"The Problem with Me Is the Problem with You" is included in *What Saves Us: Poems of Empathy and Outrage in the Age of Trump*, edited by Martín Espada.

"Self-Portrait with Dog, Possum, Newspaper, and Shovel" appeared in *The Southern Poetry Anthology, Volume VIII: Texas*, edited by William Wright and Paul Ruffin.

"The Symbolic Life" appeared in the Poem-a-Day series, on August 25, 2017.

Hayan Charara

HAYAN CHARARA is a poet, children's book author, essayist, and editor. His previous poetry books are *Something Sinister, The Sadness of Others,* and *The Alchemist's Diary.* His children's book, *The Three Lucys,* received the New Voices Award Honor, and he edited *Inclined to Speak,* an anthology of contemporary Arab American poetry. With Fady Joudah, he is also a series editor of the Etel Adnan Poetry Prize. His honors include a literature fellowship from the National Endowment for the Arts, the Lucille Joy Prize in Poetry from the University of Houston Creative Writing Program, the John Clare Prize, and the Arab American Book Award. Born in Detroit, he lived in New York City for many years before moving to Texas, where he teaches at the University of Houston. He is married, with two children.

milkweed
editions

Founded as a nonprofit organization in 1980, Milkweed Editions is an independent publisher. Our mission is to identify, nurture and publish transformative literature, and build an engaged community around it.

Milkweed Editions is based in Bdé Óta Othúŋwe (Minneapolis) within Mní Sota Makhóčhe, the traditional homeland of the Dakhóta people. Residing here since time immemorial, Dakhóta people still call Mní Sota Makhóčhe home, with four federally recognized Dakhóta nations and many more Dakhóta people residing in what is now the state of Minnesota. Due to continued legacies of colonization, genocide, and forced removal, generations of Dakhóta people remain disenfranchised from their traditional homeland. Presently, Mní Sota Makhóčhe has become a refuge and home for many Indigenous nations and peoples, including seven federally recognized Ojibwe nations. We humbly encourage our readers to reflect upon the historical legacies held in the lands they occupy.

milkweed.org

Milkweed Editions, an independent nonprofit publisher, gratefully acknowledges sustaining support from our Board of Directors; the Alan B. Slifka Foundation and its president, Riva Ariella Ritvo-Slifka; the Amazon Literary Partnership; the Ballard Spahr Foundation; *Copper Nickel*; the McKnight Foundation; the National Endowment for the Arts; the National Poetry Series; the Target Foundation; and other generous contributions from foundations, corporations, and individuals. Also, this activity is made possible by the voters of Minnesota through a Minnesota State Arts Board Operating Support grant, thanks to a legislative appropriation from the arts and cultural heritage fund. For a full listing of Milkweed Editions supporters, please visit milkweed.org.

Interior design by Tijqua Daiker and Mary Austin Speaker
Typeset in Jenson

Adobe Jenson was designed by Robert Slimbach for Adobe
and released in 1996. Slimbach based Jenson's roman styles
on a text face cut by fifteenth-century type designer
Nicolas Jenson, and its italics are based on type created by
Ludovico Vicentino degli Arrighi, a late fifteenth-century
papal scribe and type designer.